Simple Solutions

Digging

Plus Training Tips

By Kim Campbell Thornton
Illustrations by Buck Jones

BOWTIE PRESS

IRVINE, CALIFORNIA

Ruth Strother, Project Manager
Nick Clemente, Special Consultant
Michelle Martinez, Karla Austin, Editors
Michael Vincent Capozzi, Designer

The dogs in this book are referred to as *he* and *she* in alternating chapters.

Library of Congress Cataloging-in-Publication Data

Thornton, Kim Campbell.
  Digging / by Kim Campbell Thornton ; illustrations by Buck Jones.
      p. cm.
  ISBN 1-889540-95-1 (pbk. : alk. paper)
  1. Dogs--Behavior. 2. Dogs--Training. I. Title.
  SF433 .T53 2002
  636.7'0887--dc21
                              2002004410

A DIVISION OF FANCY PUBLICATIONS
3 Burroughs
Irvine, California 92618
949-855-8822

Printed and Bound in Singapore
10 9 8 7 6 5 4 3 2 1

Contents

Why Do Dogs Dig?

Are they digging to China? Looking for buried treasure? Conducting an archaeological excavation? Preparing a foundation for a new doghouse? As obsessively as some dogs dig, it certainly seems as if they must have some higher purpose for digging.

Digging is a perfectly normal behavior for dogs. Your rottweiler, Scottie, or husky isn't digging to make you angry, he's just doing what comes naturally. Some dogs are born to dig, especially the terriers, who were bred to seek out underground prey such as moles, foxes, and

badgers, and the Nordic breeds, whose ancestors dug

snow caves to keep warm in the frozen wastes of their

homeland. Digging is a remnant of the survival skills needed by ancient dogs. Before dogs became domesticated, they dug to store or find food and to create shelter for themselves and their pups. When you see your dog dig, you're watching heredity in action.

When not given other activities to occupy their minds, terriers and herding, working, or sporting dogs will dig. After all, these are dogs who were bred to have a mission, whether that was to go on rodent search-and-destroy missions, seek out and retrieve game, pull sleds or carts, herd livestock, or stand guard. They need to have a job, and if they aren't given one, well, digging will have to do.

Some dogs dig simply to mimic their owners whom they see "playing" in the dirt while gardening or doing yard work. Digging is good exercise too. It's a great workout for a dog's upper body and legs. We do aerobics, dogs dig.

Among the reasons dogs dig, entertainment, prey, shelter, attention, anxiety, and escape are the more popular. But there is a reason that dogs *don't* dig, and that's for spite. We often think that Max has dug up the yard out of revenge because we don't spend enough time with him, but, dogs just aren't programmed that way. While they're

pretty darn smart, they aren't capable of thinking, *I'll teach him to leave me alone for twelve hours straight. I'll dig a hole the size of a swimming pool!* The belief that dogs do things to get back at us is a myth that should have long since been retired.

Just because digging is normal, however, doesn't always make it acceptable. Excessive or inappropriate digging can damage or destroy yards, gardens, carpets, doors, and walls. And a dog who escapes the yard by digging is exposed to such hazards as being hit by a car, attacked by another dog, or shot by an irate neighbor, not to mention the possibilities of unwanted pregnancies or contagious diseases.

How can you stop, or at least channel, digging so that it's less destructive? Study the reasons for digging in the following chapters and ask yourself whether any of them apply to your dog. Once you've determined why Digger Dan behaves the way he does, you can use the suggestions in this book to solve your digging problem.

Digging for Fun

Digging is a lot of fun for dogs. If you think about it, a dog's digging behavior is similar to a child's enjoyment of making mud pies or finger painting. Dirt smells good when it's dug up, and tree roots can take the place of a tug toy, with the tree holding the other end of the "toy."

Dogs often dig for entertainment when they spend a lot of time alone in a yard, especially if they're left without toys. Puppies and young dogs up to three years of age dig for fun when they don't have other outlets for their energy such as regular exercise and playtime.

If your dog digs for fun, you can often redirect her energy by spending more time with her, giving her more exercise, and providing her with interesting toys. A half-hour walk once or twice a day helps your dog expend excess energy, plus it's good exercise for you too!

Puppies need even more exercise. Take yours for on-leash walks at least four times a day (after meals and naps) and provide a couple of playtime sessions in your back-yard if it's fenced so she can run off leash. Remember, just because your dog has a big yard doesn't mean she will exercise herself. Just like us, dogs need motivation, and in most cases that motivation is the presence of their people.

Dogs enjoy playing with their owners. Take some time every day to play with your dog by tossing a ball or flying

disc, playing tug, or practicing tricks or agility routines. Take an obedience class with your dog and practice the commands you learn every day, but practice for only a few minutes at a stretch. You want your dog tired, not wired.

When you can't be there to play with your dog, make sure she has several interesting toys to keep her occupied. Good choices include Kongs or Giggle Balls that are stuffed with treats, and balls of different sizes that can be rolled around the yard. Tennis balls, soccer balls, and basketballs are good choices, depending on the type of dog you have. Rotate toys so your dog always has something different to play with.

If you feed dry kibble, make your dog work for her meals. In the morning, before you leave for work, fill a Buster Cube or similar toy with the amount of food your dog gets for breakfast. The hole releases the food as the dog rolls the toy. This is your dog's big chance to hunt for her food instead of having it handed to her in a silver dog dish. The activity will keep her too busy to dig.

Provide an area where it's okay to dig and teach your dog to use it. A remote area of the yard, or any place you don't mind a few holes, is a good start. Decide on an area and allot about four square feet. Shady areas are good choices as they help your dog stay cool. A child's sandbox or a plastic wading pool are also good alternatives. Some people prefer sand because it doesn't turn into mud when it gets wet, and it's easy for the dog to shake off.

When you have decided on a digging area, cover it with about two feet of sand or loose soil. You can define or disguise the area by surrounding it with rocks, shrubs, two-by-fours, railroad ties, or even a low decorative fence. (Keep in mind that sandy, shady areas can attract fleas. Keep them at bay by mixing small amounts of diatomaceous earth (DE) in with the sand. Be careful not to breathe in the DE dust.)

Let your dog see you bury some toys or treats in the area. Encourage her to dig them up, and praise her when

she does. Keep seeding the area with interesting items so that she wants to return to it. If you catch your dog digging in a forbidden area, say, "No dig" and take her to her digging pit. Say, "Dig" in a happy tone of voice, and praise her when she does, saying, "Good dig." Providing a special digging area works best for dogs who dig for fun, not for those who dig in search of prey or to find an escape route.

If your dog just flat out prefers a hole in the ground, set up an approved digging area as described above, or learn to live with one or two holes in your yard. Taking a dog's hole away is like throwing out your spouse's favorite recliner or your comfortable mattress.

Digging for Prey

When dogs dig to pursue prey, they're just following their instincts. Their acute hearing and excellent sense of smell make them aware of underground critters such as gophers, snakes, and bugs that we're completely unaware of. Other odors dogs might smell underground are dead animals or long-buried trash. Some signs that indicate that your dog is seeking out burrowing animals, insects, or other buried treasure include a hole in a specific area (rather than at the boundary of the yard), a hole at the roots of a tree or shrub, or a trench.

Dogs who dig for prey can be more difficult to deal with because they're likely to have a never-ending supply of varmints, and they're so proud when they present you with their prize. But there are steps you can take to try to rid your yard of moles and other critters.

If your dog is hunting moles or gophers, get rid of the grubs in your yard—they're a mole's favorite food. Ask a garden shop for advice on getting rid of these varmints.

Avoid using poison to get at moles or insects; it could end up killing your dog instead of the pests.

When pest extermination isn't an option, consider confining your dog to a secure run or an area of the yard that has a concrete, wood, or brick surface. Give him plenty of toys to keep him occupied and perhaps a sandbox that he can dig in. Cover the ground inside the run with gravel, tiles, or concrete so your dog can't dig his way out. Don't forget to exercise him before he goes in the run and after he gets out.

Digging for Shelter

Dogs are den animals, and many dogs dig to provide themselves with shelter. Evidence of a shelter-digging dog is a hole the length and width of the dog's body.

Dogs usually dig near the foundation of buildings, large shade trees, or water sources. They may dig several holes around the yard so that they always have a shady place to lie as the sun moves. In hot weather, dogs dig to lie in the cool dirt, and in cold weather they may dig to build a barrier against wind. A dog who digs for this reason often lacks a doghouse or has a doghouse that's placed in an

area that's too hot or windy. Other dogs prefer to be closer to their owners, so they dig a sleeping hole that's as close to the house as possible such as under the porch.

To remedy shelter digging, provide other options to your dog for staying cool. Move the doghouse to a shady area or purchase an insulated doghouse, set up a large umbrella in the yard, or provide a child's wading pool filled with cool water. This is a great idea for water-loving dogs such as Labrador retrievers and Newfoundlands. If the weather gets really hot, let your dog stay indoors or in a cool basement. Be sure fresh drinking water is always available. In winter, provide the doghouse with warm, clean bedding and change it regularly.

Digging for Attention

Dogs who are frequently left alone dig to get attention. After all, any attention—even if it involves being yelled at—is better than none. Consider this possibility if your dog digs only when you're around or if he doesn't get much of a chance to spend time with the family.

The remedy: spend more time with your dog in the house—your dog wants to be with you. Spending ten minutes in the morning and evening with him is not enough. Your dog would much rather keep you company than dig holes by himself, even if all you're doing is watch-

ing television or puttering around the house. Dogs who feel as if they're part of the family are less likely to have behavior problems.

This means that it's important for your dog to have good house manners so you'll want him to be around. Train your dog to have manners by taking him to obedience class and practicing the commands on a regular basis. Training helps establish trust, respect, and control, and like anything else, requires regular practice and reinforcement if it's to be retained.

Besides the basic commands *sit*, *down*, *stay*, and *come*, ask the trainer to help you teach *leave it*. This command comes in handy when you want your dog to stop digging and come to you. It doesn't hurt to take a class again every year or two, just to provide socialization and learn some new things.

Consider getting a second dog to keep your dog company. The advantage of a second dog is that the two can spend hours playing with each other. The potential disadvantage is that two dogs can dig more holes than a single dog. If you decide to get a second dog, you will still need to provide toys and regular out-of-yard exercise. Also, if your first dog is a breed that is wired to dig, try to choose a second dog with a nondigging heritage.

If getting a second dog isn't an option, consider signing up your pet for doggy day care. Many boarding kennels and veterinary

MISS JONES'S DOGGY DAY CARE

offices provide this service. Day care gives your dog the opportunity to interact with other dogs and people during the day and may even provide training practice or games, such as agility and fly ball, which will wear your dog out. Not every city has doggy day care facilities, but you may be able to trade off with a neighbor or friend, or pay a local teenager to play with your dog after school.

Digging out of Anxiety

Since dogs are intelligent, social animals who need the stimulation of activity and companionship, boredom, loneliness, and isolation frequently cause destructive digging. Digging is a repetitive activity that can be comforting and help relieve anxiety, stress, or nervousness. It may even be an attempt to find the missing family. This kind of digging isn't limited to outdoor dogs; dogs left alone indoors have been known to dig into carpet or through doors or walls in an attempt to find their owners.

To help prevent separation anxiety, gradually introduce

your dog to the concept of being left alone. Start by leaving her for five or ten minutes at a time. She needs to learn that you will always come back. Slowly increase the amount of time you're gone, and be sure your dog has toys to keep her occupied. If she has a couple of favorite toys, consider making them even more special by giving them to her only when you're gone.

When you leave, do it matter-of-factly, and ignore your dog for the first few minutes upon your return. Making a big production out of leaving or arriving gives a dog the idea that being alone is bad and puts too much importance and excitement on your return. Instead, you want your dog to view arrivals and departures as routine. Fun activities such as going for a walk or being fed should be postponed until you've been home for a little while.

In extreme cases, ask your veterinarian or a qualified behaviorist for help. Behavior modification training and, if necessary, medications can be prescribed to help keep your dog calm until behavior modification techniques can work.

Digging to Escape

The psychological stress of being left alone on a regular basis can lead to phobias or anxiety that result in digging as escape behavior, such as digging through doors or escaping a boring situation by digging beneath the fence to see what or who is on the other side. Scent hounds such as beagles, bloodhounds, and coonhounds are likely to dig and escape because they want to follow any scent they catch in the air, and no puny fence is going to stop them.

Dogs who aren't altered tend to have an abundance of

sexual energy and usually dig along the fence line or under the fence to escape and find a mate. Intact males and females will climb every mountain and cross every sea

in an attempt to find a sexual companion. Sexual tension

can be lessened with the introduction of another altered

dog. To alleviate this type of digging problem, spay or neuter your dog. Along with health benefits, altered dogs are more affectionate toward their owners and less likely to wander off.

Exploration is another common canine activity that causes digging as escape behavior. Dogs explore to find food and perhaps to expand their territory. If your dog escapes to go exploring, take him on regular walks to different places to satisfy his curiosity.

More Ways to Prevent Digging

Prevent access to your dog's favorite digging areas. If she likes to dig in your garden because the turned soil has an attractive scent, fence off the area with a decorative picket fence or confine her to a run when you can't be around to supervise. It's believed that some dogs dig in gardens because they see their owners digging there. It can't hurt to put your dog in the house while you're planting your garden—just to keep her from getting any ideas.

Some dogs bury bones or other food items and later dig

them up for consumption. Try putting a halt to this by

feeding your dog indoors and only at specific times. She should get enough food for her needs but not so much that she has enough to hide for later. Pick up her food bowl twenty minutes after her meal, giving her enough time to eat but not enough time to bury a snack. Avoid giving your dog bones altogether.

How to Deter Digging

If the suggestions in this book don't work or can't be applied to your situation, the next step is to make digging a less desirable activity. There are a number of ways you can accomplish this.

Start by observing your dog, either in person or with the use of a video camera. Observing your dog will help you figure out the exact moment when your dog starts digging—information that can help you devise a solution. For instance, if you notice that your dog starts to dig after he's been left outside for half an hour, bring him inside in

twenty-five minutes. This should help short-circuit the digging behavior.

The most positive method to stop digging requires your presence. Any time you see your dog start to dig, make an unpleasant noise, such as "Aaack," to get his attention. When he stops digging, call him to you and give him a treat for coming, or grab his favorite toy and play with him. The intent is to make being with you more fun than digging.

To deter digging along the fence line, bury chicken wire at the base of the fence (with the sharp edges rolled under) or place large rocks along the bottom of the fence line. If you're installing a fence for the first time, bury the bottom of the fence one to two feet underground, or lay chain link fencing on the ground and anchor it to the bottom of the fence. This makes it uncomfortable for your dog to walk near the fence. Keep in mind, however, that these tactics won't prevent your dog from digging elsewhere in the yard.

When your dog digs in a particular spot or digs to escape, make the area unpleasant for digging by placing rocks, gravel, bricks, pinecones, or aluminum foil in the hole, or by placing chicken wire in the dirt. None of these

are pleasant digging surfaces for dogs. For a very wide

hole, try placing a metal or plastic garbage can lid inside

the hole and covering it with dirt. The noise a dog's paws make against the lid and the feel of metal or plastic may deter your digger.

You may also want to consider installing an electronic containment system that surrounds the forbidden space. While many of these systems deter a dog with an electronic shock, a new version gives off a burst of citronella spray whenever a dog wearing the collar that relays a signal to the system crosses the boundary. Citronella, a fragrant grass whose oil is often used in insect repellent, is not harmful, but dogs don't like its scent. This collar is less

severe than a shock collar and tends to be more effective.

Another tactic is to fill the holes with substances that

are unappealing to a dog's taste buds or sense of smell.

Stuff a hole with newspaper, and then sprinkle on alum, cayenne pepper, or hot sauce. The digging dog who gets a whiff or taste of these substances may think twice before beginning his next excavation project.

Electric fencing is a last resort. A low-voltage hot wire can be buried underground, around the perimeter of a fence. While an electric shock is painful, some trainers and humane organizations believe a minor shock is better for a dog than escaping and getting lost or hit by a car. Ask your trainer or behaviorist, recommended by your veterinarian, for his or her advice before installing this type of device.

Unfortunately, not every dog is deterred by these tactics. Some dogs simply view them as a challenge to overcome.

Correcting Digging Behavior

Interaction and observation is required to stop digging dogs in their tracks. First, you need to spend time with your dog and keep her entertained so that she doesn't want to dig. When you show interest in your dog, she won't resort to misbehavior for your attention. Knowing why and when your dog digs will help you eliminate her motivation for digging and redirect her digging to a more appropriate place or behavior. It's especially important that you pay close attention to your dog's outdoor activities during the first year and a half of her life. If you teach her when she's young that digging isn't permitted or that digging is permitted only in certain places, your life will be much easier.

Second, you need to correct your dog every time you catch her in the act. Any time your dog is out in the yard, use a remote correction device such as a shake can (a clean empty soda can filled with noisemakers such as pebbles or pennies with the lid taped over so the noisemakers don't fall out). Whenever you see your dog digging,

toss the can in her direction (don't hit her with it). If possible, don't let your dog see you throw the can. The noise, which should seem to come from nowhere, will startle her so that she stops digging. Distract her by giving her a toy to play with or by taking her to the preferred digging area.

A similar correction involves the use of a water hose or squirt gun. Whenever you see your dog digging, squirt her and say, "No dig." Follow this with the distraction of a toy or the introduction to a place where it's okay to dig. When she's behaving praise her by saying, "Good no dig."

If you prefer *not* to use a shake can or water correction,

simply yell, "No dig!" When she stops, praise her, give her a toy, play a game with her, or show her where she can dig. When you follow a correction with something pleasant, your dog will want to pay attention to you and follow your command.

Some dogs learn to tune out the word *no* because they hear it so frequently. If this is the case with your dog, get her attention by substituting it with a harsh sound like that of a game show buzzer, "Aaaaght."

Finally, catch your dog doing something right. Whenever you notice that she's not digging, praise her for whatever she is doing, "Good Molly to chew on your toy," or "Good Molly to play with your ball."

There are a number of corrections that are effective without being cruel. Harsh physical punishment such as hitting a dog after the fact or filling a hole with water and sticking a dog's head in it is not only abusive, but it also doesn't address the cause of the behavior or help you to form a bond with your dog. Any kind of harsh punishment can also cause dogs to become fearful or anxious or do their digging in secret. Harsh punishment doesn't communicate to your dog the reason you're punishing her; she cannot associate your anger with the hole that she's dug.

Not every solution in this book is effective with every dog. Be patient, and try different things until something works. And remember, your dog's behavior is linked to the environment and training you give her.

Kim Campbell Thornton is an award-winning writer and editor. During her tenure as editor of *Dog Fancy*, the magazine won three Dog Writers Association of America Maxwell Awards for best all-breed magazine.

Since beginning a new career in 1996 as a freelance writer, she has written or contributed to more than a dozen books about dogs and cats. Her book *Why Do Cats Do That?* was named best behavior book in 1997 by the Cat Writers Association. The companion book *Why Do Dogs Do That?* was nominated for an award by the Dog Writers Association of America. Kim serves on the DWAA Board of Governors and on the board of the Dog Writers Educational Trust. She is also president of the Cat Writers' Association and belongs to the National Writers Union.

Buck Jones's humorous illustrations have appeared in numerous magazines (including *Dog Fancy* and *Cat Fancy*) and books. He is the illustrator for the best-selling books *Barking, Chewing, House-Training, Kittens! Why Do They Do What They Do?* and *Puppies! Why Do They Do What They Do?*

For more authoritative and fun fats about dogs, including health-care advice, grooming tips, training advice, and insights into the special joys and overcoming the unique problems of dog ownership check out the latest copy of *Dog Fancy* magazine or visit the Web site at www.dogfancy.com.

BowTie Press is a division of Fancy Publications, which is the world's largest publisher of pet magazines. For more books on dogs, look for *Barking, Chewing, House-Training, Dogs Are Better Than Cats, Dogs Rule!, The Splendid Little Book of All Things Dog, Why Do Dogs Do That?* and *Puppies! Why Do They Do What They Do?* You can find all these books and more at www.bowtiepress.com.